Introduction

Sight Reading is a skill in which many people concentrate just on the _pitch_ and forget about the _rhythm_.

Most students focus primarily on getting the notes the correct pitch at the expense of keeping the beat going. However, if you look at the ABRSM marking criteria for a sight reading test, the FIRST thing that is mentioned for a distinction is, *"Fluent, rhythmically accurate"* (followed by *"accurate notes/pitch/key"*).

Sight Reading Trainer will change the way you sight read. It is not just a series of specimen sight reading tests like you can buy in the ABRSM Specimen Sight Reading Grade Books. The examples in this book are designed to be played with an accompanying audio track which can be downloaded for free at: www.music-online.org.uk/p/sight-readingtrainer.html

This will improve your rhythm and fluency when sight reading.

Another hindrance to effective sight reading is poor *"Piano Geography"*. This is the ability to feel your way around the piano *without* looking at your hands. Be honest - when you sight read, are you continually looking at your hands? It's something I call, *"watching vertical tennis"*, where your eyes travel up and down between hand and book for virtually every note or chord. *No wonder your sight reading is hesitant and lacking fluency*.

With this in mind, throughout the course there are some *"Piano Geography"* tests which *MUST BE PLAYED WITHOUT LOOKING AT YOUR HANDS.*

The third factor that will contribute to better sight reading is visualizing the music in your head (especially rhythm) before you even play a note and this includes how to use your preparation time effectively.

In an ABRSM exam for example, you are given 30 seconds to prepare. How you use this 30 seconds, is key to effective sight reading. DON'T just start playing from the beginning. Rather, the first thing you should do is get a sense of the key you are in and if you are taking an early Grade (1-2), simply find the hand position for each hand before playing a note. Throughout this course you will also find some *"Instant Hand Position or Key Signature Recognition"* tests.

Then, concentrating on the rhythm, try and visualize in your head how the music should sound, again before you even play a note. This will also include other stylistic markings such as dynamics and articulation. Getting the right pitch is only a small part of what the examiner is looking for. Below each test in this course, there will be hints of details to look out for, before you even play a note.

The last thing mentioned in the marking criteria for a distinction is "Confident presentation". A sight reading test is an assessment on how well you can convey the music as a whole performance, NOT if you can recognise the pitches A, B, C etc - that is a theory exam!!

Finally - a word on mistakes. If you do miss a note, DON'T go back and correct it, you'll only upset the flow and rhythm of the music and this effectively then counts as a 2nd mistake. You can't erase the first mistake, and the examiner is not interested if you can improve on your wrong note, he wants to hear a performance of the music as a whole, which conveys as best you can, the character of the piece.

Level 1

Equivalent to Grade 1 ABRSM / Trinity Piano Sight Reading.

In this level you will be doing tests involving hand positions limited to five notes and separate hands. For this reason, if you first concentrate on just getting the first note of each hand position correct, most of the rest of the notes should play themselves.

Key signatures will be confined to no more than one sharp or flat, so try to memorize the fact that one sharp will *always* be **F sharp**, and one flat will *always* be **B flat.** There may be occasional other accidentals as you would find in the A and D minor keys.

Rhythmically, these tests will generally contain just semibreves, dotted minims, minims, crotchets and quavers (whole, dotted half, half, quarter and eighth notes), but a couple of dotted crotchets (dotted quarter notes) at the end of the level will start preparing you for level 2.

Test 1.01

Clap the rhythm first, then put both hands in position with thumbs on the notes shown.

Test 1.02

Make sure you are aware of the jumps where the notes move by more than one step.

Test 1.03

Notice the B flat. Place your 5th finger left hand on the note shown and then a five finger run up and down including this B flat.

Test 1.04

Notice the use of dotted minims (dotted half notes) - worth 3 beats.

Piano Geography - Exercise 1

The above test must be played **without looking at your hands**. In the Audio files there are two versions, a slow one and a fast one. Make sure you can play the fast one accurately without looking down, not even once before continuing this course.

Although this is a sight reading course, **this** Piano Geography Test can be practiced as many times as you like. The purpose is to train your ability to feel your way around the keys, not train your ability to read notes.

Test 1.05

There is a key signature of B flat here. Play a five finger run in each hand and check if there are any B flats in either hand position.

Test 1.06

Make sure you are prepared for the big jumps in the first and last bar.

Test 1.07

The first half has a lot of *skips*. Be sure which are skips and which are steps.

Test 1.08

This one has some dynamics!!!

INSTANT HAND POSITION RECOGNITION EXERCISES

The following exercises give you just the first note of a potential sight reading exercise. For each one, place the correct finger on the note written, and play a simple micro scale (five finger run), in that position. The answers are given on the right of each but try to play them without any reference to the answers, maybe covering the right hand side of the page. Some of the tests that you have already done above, have had key signatures and so this exercise also includes the odd F sharp or B flat.

Test 1.09

Finger through the accidentals in the 3rd bar and be aware of the jumps at the beginning.

Test 1.10

More dynamics and accidentals to look out for.

Test 1.11

Sometimes a key signature can be a *red herring*!!

Test 1.12

Watch the *staccato* notes in bars 1 and 3.

Test 1.13

Staccato notes, slurs and dynamics - a lot to think about all together.

Test 1.14

Here there is an indication of the *mood* of the piece - sadly.

Test 1.15

What tempo does the instruction *thoughtfully* imply? Also understand where your left hand is positioned for the accidentals in the third and fourth bars.

Test 1.16

You should know the meaning of some Italian terms such as *moderato*. Which hand is affected by the F sharp key signature here?

Piano Geography - Exercise 2

In this exercise there is a key signature of *F sharp.* It is designed to help you feel the black notes without looking down. As previously the above test must be played *without looking at your hands*. In the Audio files there are two versions, a slow one and a fast one. Make sure you can play the fast one accurately without looking down, not even once before continuing this course.

Although this is a sight reading course, *this* Piano Geography Test can be practiced as many times as you like. The purpose is to train your ability to feel your way around the keys, not train your ability to read notes.

Test 1.17

Did you know the meaning of *Andante* ? Watch out for a lot of *skips*.

Test 1.18

This one introduces the dotted crotchet (dotted quarter note). Make sure the 2nd note (quavers / eighth note) in bars 1 & 3, comes in between the second and third beats.

Test 1.19

This one should go quite fast.

Test 1.20

Two contrasting sections. The first light and delicate, the second bold and emphatic. Did you notice the accents on the last two notes?

<u>Level 2</u>

Equivalent to Grade 2 ABRSM / Trinity Piano Sight Reading.

The main change at this level, is that you will be required to sight read *hands together.* Hand positions will still be confined to five notes, so as before, finding the first note of each hand position is invaluable.

Key signatures will extend to two sharps or flats. Like before you should memorize what these sharps or flats are, rather than be counting lines and spaces to identify them. Two sharps are *always* <u>**F sharp and C sharp**</u> and two flats are *always* <u>**B flat and E flat.**</u>

In addition to the dotted notes that were introduced at the end of level 1, you will now start to see tied notes. Although not really difficult to read, it is surprising how many students miss tied notes when sight reading as they are often approaching the test with a *blinkered, vertical* field of vision rather than reading *horizontally*, i.e. How one note relates to it's neighbour.

Test 2.01

From now on there will be hands together playing. Notice in this one the right hand imitates the tune of the left hand in the opening bars.

Test 2.02

Notice the key signature of F sharp, dotted rhythms and the accented notes at the end.

Test 2.03

Notice the changes of dynamics.

Test 2.04

This is the first example you have seen with a *tied note.* Also set your right hand position up carefully to cover the C sharp.

Piano Geography - Exercise 3

In this exercise there is not only a key signature of **B flat,** but also many extra accidentals. It is designed to help you get used to the feel of **changing positions** without looking down. As previously, the above test must be played **without looking at your hands,** with two audio files, a slow one and a fast one. Make sure you can play the fast one accurately without looking down, before continuing this course.

Practice this **Piano Geography Test** as many times as you like. The purpose is to train your ability to feel your way around the keys, not train your ability to read notes.

Test 2.05

Here we introduce an extra sharp into the key signature. You will need to think about F sharps and C sharps, although not necessarily both in each hand.

Test 2.06

As well as the key signature of B flat, note the extra C sharp in the third bar.

Test 2.07

Although there is not much new here, it is a bit longer than previous examples. Make sure to keep the pulse going until the end.

Test 2.08

Take advantage of the slow tempo marking *largo* to pay extra attention to the other markings, slurs, staccati and accents.

Piano Geography - Exercise 4

In this **Piano Geography** exercise you will be training to feel your way around the keys *two hands at a time.* As before, play along with the accompanying audio tracks, making sure you can do so *without looking at your hands* before continuing with the course.

Test 2.09

One common sight reading mistake is to miss tied notes as we tend to read *vertically.* Try to scan *horizontally* as you play, noticing the relationship of one note with its neighbour.

Test 2.10

This test introduces a key signature of two flats, so be aware of the E flats. Also note the F sharp in the third bar whereas the F in the first bar is natural.

Test 2.11

Another new key - E minor. Watch the D sharps in this one, as well as the key signature F sharps.

Test 2.12

The notes are not particularly hard, but it goes quite fast. Watch the timing of semiquavers and quavers (eighth notes and sixteenth notes).

INSTANT HAND POSITION RECOGNITION EXERCISES

The following exercises give you just the first note for each hand of a potential sight reading exercise. For each one, place the correct finger in each hand on the notes written, and play a simple micro scale (five finger run), in that position, with both hands together. The answers are given on the right of each but try to play them without any reference to the answers, maybe covering the right hand side of the page. Some of the tests that you have already done above, have had key signatures up to two sharps or flats and so this exercise will mirror these.

Test 2.13

Pay particular attention to the articulation in this one. The marking *leggiero* means *light* which will be brought out by the gentle staccato left hand and releasing the second note of the slurred groups in the right hand

Test 2.14

Scherzando means *playfully.* You will need to coordinate carefully the hands where one is playing staccato against the other playing legato.

Test 2.15

Sometimes a key signature will contain sharps or flats that are ***not*** relevant to the extract you are playing. Which accidental here does not apply to any of the notes you need to play? Also, prepare the left hand position particularly carefully to cover both a sharps and a flat.

Test 2.16

In this test, watch out for the "dotted quaver - semiquaver" (dotted eighth note - sixteenth note) rhythms.

Test 2.17

Pay careful attention to the articulation in this one. The playful character will be achieved by observing the staccato notes. Especially tricky is when one hand has a slur and the other a staccato at the same time.

Test 2.18

Another test in E minor. This time however, there are *two* extra accidentals, D sharp *and* C sharp.

Level 3

Equivalent to Grade 3 ABRSM / Trinity Piano Sight Reading.

The main change at this level, is that hand positions will now extend beyond five notes and can change during the tests. This makes it important to have a sense of what key you are in, rather than just doing a five finger run in one five note position. With this in mind, a good idea at this level is to quickly play a one octave scale of the key you are in, being aware not only of the key signature, but also whether it is a major *or* relative minor with the same key signature. Minor keys are often identified immediately by their *extra accidentals.*

To summarize, by this level you should know *from memory* the following:

No Key Signature - C major / A minor
One sharp - G major / E minor
Two sharps - D major / B minor
Three sharps - A   major / (F sharp minor)*
One flat - F major / D minor
Two flats - B flat major / G minor
Three flats - E flat major / (C minor)*

* The two scales in brackets are shown here are to complete the pattern of relative minors but will not be tested at this level

The other element that will be introduced at this level is two note chords in one hand or the other, but not both hands at the same time.

Test 3.01

Hand positions may change during the piece from now on. The suggested fingering will ensure your thumb finishes on the bottom G enabling a smooth legato octave slur at the end.

Test 3.02

In bars 1-4, the right hand mainly stays in one position apart from the first note (where the right hand thumb will be extended slightly out to the E) and the last note where "3" crosses over to make the new hand position of the last two bars.

Test 3.03

There are multiple hand position changes in this one, especially in the right hand. A little hint - after the initial finger numbers on the first notes of each hand, any subsequent finger numbers on the music will indicate a *change* in hand position.

Piano Geography - Exercise 5

In this **Piano Geography** exercise you will be training to feel your way around the keys *in extended hand positions.* Remember that a written fingering on the test is usually a good clue that there is a change of hand position.

As before, play along with the accompanying audio tracks, making sure you can do so *without looking at your hands* before continuing with the course.

Test 3.04

Notice a new key signature here - that of E flat major. It might be an idea to run through a one octave scale of E flat major just to let your hands get a feel for the accidentals of this key.

Test 3.05

This is yet another new key for this level - B minor although it has the same key signature of two sharps, as its relative major (D major that you have already come across). Again, it is a good idea to play a one octave scale of the key you are in to get your hands familiar with the accidentals in this key. Speed will be governed by the marking *Doloroso* which hopefully you know means *sadly*.

Test 3.06

Particular attention needs to be paid to the first half where one hand plays staccato whilst the other hand has more sustained notes.

Piano Geography - Exercise 6
(Observe fingerings EXACTLY)

In this **Piano Geography** exercise you will be practicing changing hand positions by **crossing thumbs under** or **crossing over thumbs.** Remember that a written fingering on the test is usually a good clue that there is a change of hand position.

As before, play along with the accompanying audio tracks, making sure you can do so **without looking at your hands** before continuing with the course.

Test 3.07

The tempo marking *allegretto* needs to be taken a little faster than most of the previous examples. Note again the key signature of E flat major and the sneaky tied note at the end.

Test 3.08

The staccato notes, quiet dynamic, B minor key signature and the marking *sneakily* all give you clues of how to play this test.

Test 3.09

The marking *Pesante* requires a heavy touch. Notice the tenuto markings on the longer chords. They need to be long but slightly separated.

Piano Geography - Exercise 7

In this *Piano Geography* exercise you will be training to feel your way around *two note chords*. Practice this exercise as many times as necessary to make sure you can navigate all the position changes by touch only.

As before, play along with the accompanying audio tracks, making sure you can do so *without looking at your hands* before continuing with the course.

Test 3.10

Some playful staccato is needed to bring out the *scherzando* marking.

Test 3.11

Remember, the printed fingerings often give a clue of where to expect hand position changes. In your preparation, make sure the right hand shape of bar 4 is fixed in your visualization.

Test 3.12

There are some quick hand position changes for the left hand which you might want to practice first of all. Also be careful when one hand is marked *staccato* and the other is *legato.*

INSTANT KEY SIGNATURE RECOGNITION EXERCISES
<u>LEVEL 3</u>

The following exercises give you just the first bar of a potential sight reading exercise. ***Do not play*** the notes in the test, but rather play a one octave hands together *scale of the key* that the notes are in. This is a good habit to get into for preparation of sight reading tests. Answers are given at the end.

1.

2.

3.

4.

5.

6.

7.

8.

9.

10.

Answers:
1. D minor 2. G minor 3. E flat major 4. D major 5. F major
6. B minor 7. B flat major 8. G major 9. E minor 10. A major

Test 3.13

Tests will now start to get longer. Notice in this one there is a key signature of E flat major, some two note chords and don't get caught out by the tied notes.

Test 3.14

Dotted quaver - semiquaver (dotted eighth note - sixteenth note) rhythms feature in this one. Make sure the semiquaver (sixteenth note) does not just become a lazy triplet quaver (triplet eighth note).

Test 3.15

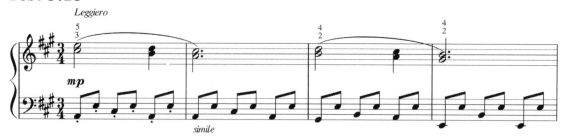

Watch the staccato left hand against a legato right hand at the beginning.

Test 3.16

Another eight bar melody, this time in 4/4 time making it the longest so far in this book. Notice the B minor key signature with it's extra raised A sharps.

Test 3.17

This waltz type test should flow quite legato at the beginning, but notice the change of articulation in the last two bars where there is a *crescendo* into a ***staccato forte*** finish. Also be careful to observe the rests where they are marked.

Test 3.18

A new time signature of 3/8 with dotted rhythms is introduced here. Watch out for the tied note in the right hand at the end of bar 4.

Test 3.19

Hands work quite independently on this one and watch out for the two note chords and accidentals.

Test 3.20

For the final test at level 3, here is one that has a two note chord in either one hand or the other on every beat. Also watch the modulation to B minor on the second line.

Level 4

Equivalent to Grades 4 & 5 ABRSM / Trinity Piano Sight Reading.

At this level, tests will now move onto four sharps or flats. As with level 3, a good way to prepare a sight reading test is to initially play a single octave scale of the key that the test is in. At this point you should know from memory and instantly, all the following keys:

No Key Signature - C major / A minor
One sharp - G major / E minor
Two sharps - D major / B minor
Three sharps - A   major / F sharp minor
Four sharps - E major / C sharp minor
One flat - F major / D minor
Two flats - B flat major / G minor
Three flats - E flat major / C minor
Four flats - A flat major / F minor

Other features that you may come across in the tests from now on are:
● More chromatic notes
● Syncopation
● Pause and tenuto signs
● Changes of speed - especially slowing down at the end of a test.
● Two note chords in both hands at the same time.

Test 4.01

This test is essentially in A minor, but there are a few *chromatic notes,* especially the E flats that are not part of the key and which give it a jazzy bluesy feel. Be aware that the 4th bar left hand is not F sharp anymore.

Test 4.02

The best preparation for a piece like this is to finger through the chromatic sections such as the LH bars 3 and 4.

Test 4.03

This test introduces an *anacrusis* or *upbeat*. Notice also the key signature of E flat major although in bar 6, there is an A natural, which is not in this key. The audio track will count in 1,2, 3, 1, 2..

Test 4.04

Things to watch out for in this test include the tied note in bar 4, the variation away from the key signature in bar 6 and the rhythm of bar 7.

Test 4.05

Be careful that some F's are sharp and others are not. Imagine the dotted rhythms in your head before even touching the keyboard. To get a good legato left hand, observe the fingering suggestions at the beginning.

Test 4.06

This is the first test with a 6/8 key signature. As indicated at the start, aim for a very flowing melody, ensuring especially that each group of triplet quavers (eighth notes) moves smoothly onto the following dotted crotchet (quarter note) in each case.

Test 4.07

As indicated by the marking *Tempo di Minuetto,* try to aim for the character of a courtly dance in this test. Although basically in D minor, watch out for the odd suprise accidental.

Piano Geography Exercise 8

In this ***Piano Geography*** exercise you will be training to feel your way around ***parallel octaves.*** Practice this exercise as many times as necessary to make sure you can navigate all the position changes by touch only.

As before, play along with the accompanying audio tracks, making sure you can do so ***without looking at your hands*** before continuing with the course.

Test 4.09

Another test in 6/8 time, but the tempo is somewhat faster as you will notice when playing with the accompanying audio track. Watch out for the chromatic left hand notes.

Test 4.10

This test is actually very similar to 4.03   but with a much more flowing bass line. Watch out for the rather *stretchy* left hand position in bar 2.

Test 4.11

Quite a lot of hand position changes here. Ideally, try to make these without looking down at your hands as your sense of piano geography develops.

Test 4.12

One of the new things introduced at this level will be the use of syncopation. Have a clear idea in your head how the rhythms of the opening bars should sound and be careful when the left hand plays on the beat under a tied note in the Right Hand (e.g. Bars 3, 5 and 6)

Test 4.13

Andante Sostenuto

It might be an idea to play a one octave scale that corresponds to the key signature of this one, before you start. This will be the first time you've used this key in this course.

Test 4.14

Lilting

Don't be put off by the dissonances in this piece, on the contrary, relish them. Also be aware that many, if not all the B's are natural as one would expect in this key of C minor. The rhythms of bars 6 and 7 don't follow the expected pattern of the previous bars and could catch you out if you're not careful.

INSTANT KEY SIGNATURE RECOGNITION EXERCISES
LEVEL 4

The following exercises give you just the first bar of a potential sight reading exercise. ***Do not play*** the notes in the test, but rather play a one octave hands together ***scale of the key*** that the notes are in. This is a good habit to get into for preparation of sight reading tests.

Answers are given at the end.

1.

2.

3.

4.

5.

6.

7.

8.

9.

10.

ANSWERS:
1. E major   2. C minor   3. E flat major   4. A flat major   5. F minor
6. B minor   7. B flat major   8. F sharp minor   9. C sharp minor   10. A major

Test 4.15

This test relies on careful articulation to really bring out the character of the piece. Notice in bars 1, 3 and 5 how the right hand has a tenuto note whilst the left hand has a staccato note. There are also some tricky accidentals in bar 6. Any preparation time would be wisely spent on this section first.

Test 4.16

It can be easy to be put off by dissonance. Here you must play the clashing notes, as instructed at the beginning, **boldly.** This test is also the first time you have come across a **ritardando** marking. Additionally, spend a moment making sure you have identified the pitch of the final chord.

Test 4.17

Although not difficult in theory, many students don't pay attention to rests in sight reading tests. There are plenty here. Notice too the delicate **staccato / pianissimo** ending.

Test 4.18

In this test watch out for:
1) two note chords in both hands at the same time
2) a **ritardando** at the end.

Test 4.19

Notice the instruction **"With an easy Latin feel."** Although, not too fast, you'll need to be rhythmically on your toes for this one. Also don't get caught out by the F's in bar 7 where you might be expecting E flats in the left hand.

Test 4.20

For the final test in level 4, try this exercise involving two note chords in both hands throughout the piece. There are also some surprising twists of chromatic harmony and unexpected key changes.

Level 5

Equivalent to Grades 6-8 ABRSM / Trinity Piano Sight Reading.

At this level, tests will now move onto five sharps or flats. As with level 4, a good way to prepare a sight reading test is to initially play a single octave scale of the key that the test is in. At this point you should know *from memory* and *instantly* all the following keys:

No Key Signature - C major / A minor
One sharp - G major / E minor
Two sharps - D major / B minor
Three sharps - A   major / F sharp minor
Four sharps - E major / C sharp minor
Five sharps - B major / G sharp minor
One flat - F major / D minor
Two flats - B flat major / G minor
Three flats - E flat major / C minor
Four flats - A flat major / F minor
Five flats - D flat major / B flat minor

Other features that you may come across in the tests from now on are:
● Changes of Clef
● Use of pedals
● 8va sign
● Changes of speed in the middle of a piece (not just a final rit)
● Three note chords in both hands at the same time.

Test 5.01

At Level 5 we will start to introduce the right pedal into these tests. This one is fairly slow, so concentrate on making the quavers flowing at the beginning, but notice the changes in articulation in bars 5, 6 and 8 with the addition of a couple of staccato notes.

Test 5.02

Notice how the different hands have different dynamic markings. Try to make the right hand - *"cantabile"* above the softer left hand. Be careful also of pedal changes.

Test 5.03

In this test, 9/8 time is introduced. To capture the character of this piece, careful attention needs to paid to the articulation markings.

Test 5.04

Try to bring out the melody of the right hand keeping the left hand chords, supportive, but not distracting in this sustained expressive test.

Piano Geography Exercise 9

In this **Piano Geography** exercise you will be training to feel your way around **three note chords.** Although three note chords do not really get tested in ABRSM sight reading until grade 8, these examples are quite straight forward and should be achievable by a grade 6 student.

Practice this exercise as many times as necessary to make sure you can navigate all the position changes by touch only.

As before, play along with the accompanying audio tracks, making sure you can do so **without looking at your hands** before continuing with the course.

Test 5.05

The new key signature of F minor, should not cause too many problems, however you might want to spend a few moments of your preparation time on the parallel thirds of the second half. Pedalling should be done once per bar as indicated by the *simile* marking. Notice also the **ritardando** at the end.

Test 5.06

At this level you need to use the 8va sign. Take care setting your right hand up in the correct position and notice how the tempo will ease off coming to a rest on the very quiet pause on the last note.

Test 5.07

You will need very careful counting in this one. Think of the 7/8 time signature as being a group of three quavers (such as the compound beat of 6/8 time), followed by two crotchets. It might help to count "*1, 2, 3, 1, +, 2, +*" with the stresses on the numbers in bold.

Test 5.08

Above all, note the tempo marking *Tempo di Minuetto*. This needs to sound like a dance. Be aware of the clef changes in bars 9 & 11 and also the *Ritardando / A Tempo* markings in bars 11 & 12.

Test 5.09

The marking ***Doloroso con rubato*** at the beginning implies that
you need to have some freedom of time with this test. In the audio
recordings that accompany this book, there is a slight easing of the
tempo in bar 8 as well as the marked ***ritardando*** at the end. Also be
aware of the change of clef in the middle.

Piano Geography - Exercise 10

Pedal once per bar so you can release LH early

In this *Piano Geography* exercise you will be training to feel your way around *leaping between bass notes and three note chords.* As suggested on the music above, use some pedal, once per bar so that you can release the left hand early and have more time to jump to the chord.

Practice this exercise as many times as necessary to make sure you can navigate all the position changes by touch only.

As before, play along with the accompanying audio tracks, making sure you can do so *without looking at your hands* before continuing with the course.

Test 5.10

Keep dotted rhythms very crisp and watch out for the ***tempo changes*** in the middle.

Test 5.11

Three note chords have already been practiced in the ***Piano Geography*** exercises, but this is their first occurrence in a sight reading test. Notice the two contrasting styles in this test:
1) The legato running quavers (eighth notes)as in the first two bars
2) The staccato quavers in between the block chords.

Note the *simile* marking, indicating to continue these two styles throughout the test.

Test 5.12

Notice the use of pedal and the change of tempo at the end. Make use of the accents to achieve a jazzy style and observe the two note slurs in bar 8.

Test 5.13

The opening uses some basic A flat major shapes, preparation time would be best spcnt on the second line which starts in ***C flat major*** but it might be easier to think of the enharmonic equivalent here - B major. Notice the ***poco rit*** in bar 6 which you can use to your advantage in preparing the tricky chords of the third beat and final bar.

INSTANT KEY SIGNATURE RECOGNITION EXERCISES
LEVEL 5

The following exercises give you just the first bar of a potential sight reading exercise. ***Do not play*** the notes in the test, but rather play a one octave hands together ***scale of the key*** that the notes are in. This is a good habit to get into for preparation of sight reading tests.

As a guide, five sharps only comes into ABRSM sight reading tests at grade 8, with grades 5-7 employing just four sharps or flats. Seeing as this exercise comes near the end of the final level in this course, you should now be able to recognise a key instantly up to 5 sharps or flats.

Answers are given at the end.

5.

6.

7.

8.

9.

10.

Answers
1. B major   2. B minor   3. E flat major   4. F sharp minor   5. F minor
6. C minor   7. B flat major   8. A flat major   9. C sharp minor   10. D flat major

Test 5.14

This extract has many details that need to be noticed, including for the first time in this course, **spread chords**. Other items to be aware of are the changes in tempo, the pause signs and the octave signs. However, you can make use of the **espressivo** marking, playing it at quite a relaxed tempo, thus giving yourself time to absorb all these details.

Test 5.15

Although this piece is not technically difficult, it does use a new key signature of D flat major, which you hadn't previously encountered in these tests.

Test 5.16

Another new key signature of five sharps, along with tempo changes, double sharps, pedalling and an *"8va **higher**"* notation at the end will give you plenty to think about in this test.

Test 5.17

A nice playful tempo with crisp staccato notes and double grace notes are needed to bring out the ***giocoso*** character of this piece, Watch out for the sudden changes of tonality, B flat major to B major and back again, in bars 4 and 10.

Test 5.18

Make sure of the rhythm in the 5/4 bars, where the quavers (eighth notes) follow a 3-3-4 pattern. Also note that in these bars the left hand will be playing on top of the right hand. Also don't gct caught out by the clef change for the right hand in bar 6.

Test 5.19

Quite hymn like in it's character, aim for an efficient use of pedal to achieve legato chord progressions. You should be getting used to the five flat key signature by now and the use of four note chords for much of the piece and even a couple of five note chords at the end.

Made in the USA
Las Vegas, NV
05 July 2023

74242958R00042